D1633380

THE BEST
OF CANARY ISLANDS
COOKERY

THE BEST
OF CANARY ISLANDS
COOKERY

FELISA VERA
REMEDIOS SOSA
ANA LEAL
YURENA DÍAZ

© AUTHORS
© CENTRE OF CANARIAN CULTURE

Supervision the editions: C. Otero Alonso

Translated by: Pauline Agnew

Cover photographs: "Poached viejas", from the Obra Social of Caja Canarias

Cover desing: Centre of Canarian Culture

Composition: Laura López

Film Service: *TALLER RELAX*
      Urb. Guajara, 83
      La Laguna. Santa Cruz de Tenerife

Printing: FARESO, S. A.
      Paseo de la Dirección, 5
      28039 Madrid

ISBN: 84-7926-092-0

Legal Deposit n.º: M. 24.840-1992

PRESENTATION

As its title indicates, the aim of "Selected Recipes from the Canary Islands" is to compile the most representative recipes of Canarian cuisine using, of course, the typical products of the islands.

We shall therefore see that this type of gastronomy is characteristic of the region and that it differs from the rest of Spanish cuisine both in the cooking methods and the ingredients employed.

With regard to the vocabulary used in this book, we would like to explain some of the names of the utensils used by the islanders and which are not likely to be known by those who are unfamiliar with our cuisine.

The two most important are:

- **Lebrillo**: a large deep circular earthenware dish like a baking bowl, used for serving at table in Canarian homes.

- **Milana:** a shallow rectangular tin tray, used for cooking certain desserts in the oven. In La Gomera it is known as a "vilana" and gives its name to the "Torta Vilana".

The use of certain types of dishes is recommended in some of the recipes, but any plate or dish of similar characteristics may be employed.

We should also point out that certain ingredients have different names, depending on the area from which they come; the "batata" or sweet potato, for example, is called "boniato" in La Palma, and the herb "hortelana" (mint) is known in some places as "hierbabuena" or "hierbahuerto". Frequently used ingredients include "pimentón", which is powdered dried red pimentos and is the same as paprika.

Cumin and aniseed are used in seed form and sugar is granulated in all the recipes given in this book, unless otherwise stated.

We are indebted to the many friends who have helped make this book possible, and in particular to Carmen Delia Leal, Elizabeth Ramos, Flora Lilia Barrera and María del Carmen Otero.

Finally, the amounts of the ingredients given in the recipes are calculated approximately to serve four. Where no specific amount has been stated in a particular case in the original version of this book it is because most Canarians would be familiar with the end product and common sense would dictate the quantity to use. May the readers of this English version use their common sense successfully and enjoy the fruits of their labours!

SOPA DE MARISCOS
(Seafood soup)

You will need:

Different types of seafood: medium sized and small crabs, limpets, winkles and mussels; a piece of fish and the head, 3 tomatoes, 1 onion, 1 clove garlic, "pimentón" (powdered dried red pimentos, the same as paprika), parsley, saffron, 1 green pepper, mint, 1 small glass rice, oil and salt.

Preparation:

Clean the seafood, removing beards and barnacles. Chop the onion, tomatoes, green pepper and parsley and gently fry in the oil together with the piece of fish and the head, if included, until the fish is golden.

Crush the garlic in a mortar with a little salt, 1 or 2 threads of saffron (easier to crush if previously "toasted" briefly in a warm place such as the cooker lid) and a teaspoonful of pimentón. Add this, together with the remainder of the seafood, to the fried ingredients and put this mixture into a saucepan containing boiling water and a sprig of mint.

Bring to the boil for a while and then strain. Add the rice to the stock, then the flaked fish and other cooked seafood and simmer over moderate heat until the rice is tender.

9

SOPA DE AJOS
(Garlic soup)

You will need:
    1 head garlic, 1/2 large glass oil, 1 small loaf, sliced, 1 egg per person and salt.

Preparation:

    Peel the garlic and pound in a mortar. Fry quickly in a little oil in a saucepan, taking care not to burn.
    Add the necessary water and salt and bring to the boil.
    Fry the slices of bread and add to the saucepan. Just before removing from the heat, add the raw eggs and stir gently. They will set in the hot soup.

PUCHERO
(Vegetable stew)

You will need:
200 grs chick-peas, 500 grs beef, 500 grs pork, 1 kg cabbage, 200 grs pumpkin, 1 chayote, 200 grs French beans, 1 fresh corncob, 1 sweet potato, 1 kg potatoes, 2 or 3 small firm pears, 30 grs vegetable marrow, 1 or 2 carrots, 1 leek, 1 head garlic, 1 onion, 1 tomato, saffron, thyme and salt.

Preparation:

Soak the chick-peas in cold water overnight.

Drain and put in a large saucepan with the meat and cover well with water. Chop the leek, onion and tomato and add to the saucepan, together with the thyme, saffron and the garlic, which has been pounded in a mortar with the salt.

When these ingredients are cooked, add the remaining vegetables, cut in large pieces, with the exception of the French beans which are left whole and tied together with a string.

Simmer until all ingredients are tender.

The stock can be used to prepare soup and a dish called "escaldón", the recipe for the latter being included later on in this book.

11

The vegetables are arranged on a serving dish (without the stock), and can be accompanied by a typical sauce made with fresh coriander, known as "mojo de cilantro".

ROPA VIEJA
(Beef or pork stew)

You will need:

500 grs chick-peas, 1 kg potatoes, 500 grs beef or pork, 500 grs chicken or hen, 1 small glass cooking wine, 2 tomatoes, 1 onion, 1 green pepper, 3 cloves garlic, thyme, 1 bay leaf, 2 or 3 threads saffron, parsley, black peppercorns, pimentón and salt.

Preparation:

Soak the chick-peas overnight in cold water.

Add the drained chick-peas with the meat and chicken to a saucepan of boiling water and salt to taste. Once tender, drain off the stock. Chop the meat and the chicken.

Fry the chopped onion, tomatoes and pepper together in a frying-pan with a little oil, adding the mixture of the garlic and peppercorns which has previously been crushed in a mortar, together with a teaspoonful of pimentón, the saffron and a little salt. When almost cooked, add the wine, parsley, bay leaf, thyme, chick-peas and meat and cook for a further few minutes. Keep warm.

Dice and fry the potatoes and combine them with the fried mixture. Serve hot.

13

POTAJE DE LENTEJAS
(Lentil pottage)

You will need:
500 grs lentils, 500 grs pumpkin, 500 grs potatoes, 2 corncobs, 1 thick slice bacon or piece of cooking chorizo (red sausage), 1 onion, 2 or 3 medium tomatoes, 3 cloves garlic, 1 green pepper, oil, saffron, pimentón, oil and salt.

Preparation:

Rinse the lentils in cold running water after removing any small stones or grit. Peel and dice the pumpkin, potatoes, onion, tomatoes and green pepper and place with the lentils in a large saucepan with sufficient cold water. Add the sliced corncobs and chopped bacon. Peel and finely chop the garlic and add to the saucepan.

Finally, add a small glass of oil, half a teaspoonful of pimentón, the 2 or 3 threads of saffron and salt to taste.

Bring to the boil and then simmer until cooked, taking care to stir occasionally.

POTAJE DE COLES VERDES
(Cabbage pottage)

You will need:
1 green cabbage, 500 grs red beans, 250 grs salted pork ribs, 2 kgs potatoes, 1 head garlic, pimentón, 1 onion, 2 tomatoes, 1/2 green pepper, oil and salt.

Preparation:

Soak the red beans in cold water overnight.

Drain and place the beans in a large saucepan of cold water with the rinsed pork ribs and bring to the boil. Finely chop the cabbage, onion, tomatoes and pepper and add with the coarsely chopped potatoes. Crush the garlic with salt, pimentón and a little oil and add to the saucepan. Simmer until tender.

POTAJE DE JARAMAGOS

(The characteristic ingredient of this pottage is a yellow-flowered weed of cultivated fields known as "jaramagos"and belonging to the family of the radish, of which only the leaves are used).

You will need:

500 grs jaramago leaves, 2 kgs potatoes, 500 grs pumpkin, 500 grs white beans, 500 grs lean pork, 500 grs sweet potato, 500 grs yam (if desired), 2 or 3 tomatoes, 1 onion, 3 cloves garlic, pimentón, cumin, oil, 2 or 3 threads saffron and salt.

Preparation:

Place the beans and meat in a large saucepan of cold water and begin to heat.

Boil the jaramago leaves in a different saucepan to avoid giving the stew a bitter taste.

When the beans are parboiled, add the drained, chopped jaramago leaves and chopped pumpkin, potatoes, sweet potato, tomatoes and onion, with a small glass of oil. Crush the garlic in a mortar with a little cumin, the saffron, a teaspoonful pimentón and a little salt and stir into the saucepan. Simmer until tender.

16

POTAJE DE BUBANGOS
(Courgette pottage)

You will need:
3 courgettes, 250 grs pumpkin, 2 carrots, 1 kg potatoes, 1 onion, 2 cloves garlic, 1 corncob, thyme, oil and salt.

Preparation:

Peel or scrape and dice the courgettes. Place them in a large saucepan with the diced pumpkin, carrots, potatoes and the sliced corncob and cover well with cold water. Add the chopped onion, garlic and parsley and a sprig of thyme, with oil and salt to taste. Stir occasionally and simmer until tender.

POTAJE DE ACELGAS
(Kale pottage)

You will need:
500 grs kale, 250 grs chick-peas, 500 grs pumpkin, 1 kg potatoes, 250 grs salted pork ribs, 1 corncob, 1 onion, 2 or 3 tomatoes, 2 cloves garlic, 2 or 3 threads saffron, pimentón, oil and salt.

Preparation:

Soak the chick-peas and salted pork ribs separately in cold water overnight.

Bring a saucepan of water to the boil and add the chick-peas, the ribs and the washed and chopped kale. Add the chopped pumpkin, potatoes, onion, tomatoes and garlic and the sliced corncob. Stir in a little oil, salt to taste, a teaspoonful of pimentón and the saffron and simmer until tender.

POTAJE DE BERROS
(Watercress pottage)

You will need:
500 grs watercress, 250 grs white beans, 1 1/2 kgs potatoes, 250 grs salted pork, 1 corncob, 1 onion, 1 tomato, 2 or 3 cloves garlic, 1 green pepper, 2 or 3 threads saffron and oil.

Preparation:

Soak the beans and the salted pork separately in cold water overnight.

Drain and place in a large saucepan, cover well with cold water and bring to the boil, at which point a glass of cold water is added to "scare" the beans! Next add the finely chopped watercress with the meat and the corncob. Simmer for a while before adding the diced potatoes and the chopped onion, tomato and green pepper. Crush the garlic and mix into the soup, adding a little oil and the powdered saffron. Salt to taste. Simmer until tender.

It is customary in the islands to serve this soup with a good "escaldón" (separate recipe), fresh white cheese and chopped onion.

POTAJE DE LECHE
(Milk pottage)

You will need:

1 kg calabash, 1 kg sweet potato, 500 grs potatoes, 1 or 2 corncobs, 250 grs pumpkin, milk, 1 small glass rice, sugar and salt.

Preparation:

Chop all the vegetables and combine with the corn grains in a saucepan with a little water and a sprinkling of salt.

Parboil the rice with twice its volume of water and a little milk. Add to the vegetable and corn mixture and simmer until all the ingredients are tender. Add sufficient milk to cover the surface of the mixture and sprinkle with a little sugar. Bring to the boil and remove from the heat immediately so that the milk does not curdle.

POTAJE DE GARBANZOS
(Chick-pea pottage)

You will need:
500 grs chick-peas, 250 grs pork ribs, 1 1/2 kgs potatoes, 1 corncob, 1 onion, 1/2 head garlic, pimentón and salt.

Preparation:

Soak the chick-peas and the pork ribs separately in cold water overnight.

Drain both these ingredients and cook together in salted water. Dice the potatoes, slice the corncob, chop the onion and garlic, and add to the saucepan with some oil and a teaspoonful of pimentón. Bring to the boil and simmer until tender.

ALMOGROTE
(Cheese spread)

You will need:
500 grs hard goatsmilk cheese, 500 grs ripe tomatoes, 6 cloves garlic, 1 hot pepper, oil and salt.

Preparation:

Remove the seeds and veins from the pepper and pound it in a mortar with the garlic and a little salt.

Peel the tomatoes and remove the seed. Mash the pulp with a fork.

Mix well with the contents of the mortar.

Grate the cheese and combine with the tomato and garlic mixture, adding olive oil and beating continually until a smooth paste is formed.

MOJO DE QUESO
(Cold cheese sauce)

You will need:
500 grs hard goatsmilk cheese, 4 cloves garlic, 1 green pepper, cumin and salt.

Preparation:

Remove the seeds and veins from the pepper. Pound the pepper, garlic, salt to taste and cumin in a mortar.

Grate the cheese and mix with the contents of the mortar. Add water and olive oil to form a well-blended liquid.

MOJO COLORADO
(Red sauce)

You will need:
3 or 4 hot red peppers, 1 small head garlic, cumin, oil, vinegar, pimentón and salt.

Preparation:

Lightly toast 1/2 teaspoon of cumin and pound in a mortar.

Soften the peppers by soaking for a while in hot water. Remove the seeds and veins. Add to the mortar and pound with the cumin.

Put the garlic and salt into the mortar and crush with the contents, adding a small glass of oil, vinegar to taste and a little cold water. Blend well and serve.

Another red sauce which is similar although not so "hot" is prepared as follows: lightly toast 2 or 3 threads of locally grown saffron and pound in a mortar with breadcrumbs soaked in olive oil, garlic, cumin, pimentón and salt. Add a little more oil, vinegar to taste and half a teaspoonful of pimentón, blending thoroughly.

MOJO VERDE
(Green sauce)

You will need:
3 or 4 hot green peppers, 1 small head garlic, cumin, parsley, oil, vinegar and salt.

Preparation:

Put the following ingredients into a mortar and pound together: a teaspoon of cumin, the garlic and salt to taste. Remove the seeds and veins from the peppers and add with some chopped parsley to the mortar. Pound the contents thoroughly. Finally, combine with some oil, vinegar to taste and water.

MOJO DE CILANTRO
(Coriander sauce)

You will need:
1 head garlic, 1/2 hot red or green pepper, 1 bunch fresh coriander, cumin, oil, vinegar and salt.

Preparation:

Lightly toast a teaspoon of cumin and pound in a mortar. Add the garlic, coriander, seeded pepper and a little salt, blending all these ingredients thoroughly. Pour in half a cup of oil, vinegar to taste, a little cold water and mix well.

LENTEJAS COMPUESTAS
(Lentil stew)

You will need:

500 grs lentils, 1 onion, 3 tomatoes, 3 cloves garlic, 1 green pepper, 1 small glass cooking wine, 200 grs piece of fat bacon, 1 egg per person, cooking chorizo (red sausage), 3 black peppercorns, thyme, 1 or 2 bay leaves, pimentón, olive oil and salt.

Preparation:

Separate any small stones, etc., from the lentils, which have preferably been soaked overnight in cold water. Cut the piece of bacon into small pieces and place in a large saucepan with the lentils and abundant water. Bring to the boil, stirring frequently so that the lentils do not stick to the bottom of the saucepan and add water if necessary.

Prepare a typical Canarian "fritura" or "fried mixture" by chopping the onion, tomatoes and green pepper and frying these ingredients together in a suitable amount of oil. Pound in a mortar the garlic, the 3 peppercorns and some cooking salt. Add this to the frying-pan with the thyme, bay leaf, the peeled and sliced chorizo and the wine. Stir well.

Add the contents of the frying-pan to the lentils and cook over gentle heat until the lentils are tender but whole.

27

Garnish each serving with a triangle of fried bread and wedges of hardboiled egg.

CALDO DE PAPAS Y HUEVOS
(Potato and egg soup)

You will need:
  2 kgs potatoes, 1 onion, 2 tomatoes, 2 cloves garlic, 1 leek (optional), 1 egg per person, parsley, fresh coriander, pimentón, 2 or 3 threads saffron, oil and salt.

Preparation:

  Peel and dice the potatoes. Finely chop the onion, tomatoes, leek and parsley. Place all the above ingredients in a saucepan, add a small glass of oil, a sprig of coriander, a teaspoonful of pimentón and the garlic previously pounded with the salt.
  Sauté this mixture until golden, then cover with water and bring to the boil. Once the potatoes are cooked, stir 1 beaten egg into the soup. Break the remaining eggs on the surface and allow to set.

PAPAS CON PIÑAS Y COSTILLA
(Potatoes with corncobs and pork ribs)

You will need:
2 kgs potatoes, 1 kg salted pork ribs, and 4 or 5 tender corncobs.

Preparation:

Soak the ribs overnight in cold water.

Drain and cut the ribs into several portions and place in a saucepan with fresh water. Add the sliced corncobs. Bring to the boil and cook until tender. Add the peeled potatoes, cutting large ones in half.

Drain off the stock and reserve when the potatoes are boiled and place the food on a serving dish. Serve with coriander sauce (optional but highly recommended), some "gofio", mixed with some of the reserved stock and shaped into balls the size of a golfball, and any good local wine.

Note: "Gofio" used to be an important part of the staple diet of the Canarians and is still a popular garnish for the typical dishes. It is a flour obtained by toasting and grinding different types of grain, either together or separately, the most widely used being corn.

PAPAS VIUDAS
("Widowed" potatoes)

You will need:
 1 1/2 kgs potatoes, 3 tomatoes, 2 onios, 1 green pepper, 6 cloves garlic, 1 egg per person, white wine, parsley, thyme, bay leaf, olive oil and salt.

Preparation:

 Peel and slice the potatoes. Boil in salted water and drain.

 Prepare a typical "fritura" (fried mixture) by frying the chopped onions, tomatoes and green pepper in the oil, adding a sprig of thyme, the bay leaf, parsley and crushed garlic, with salt to taste.

 When the fritura is tender, add a glass of wine and stir well. Pour this over the drained potatoes. Boil briefly and turn off heat. Serve hot with wedges of boiled egg.

 This recipe can also be used with fresh or frozen peas instead of potatoes.

PAPAS ARRUGADAS
("Wrinkled potatoes")

You will need:
2 kgs medium or small potatoes, 5 dessertspoons cooking salt, 1 large cabbage leaf.

Preparation:

Wash the potatoes well and put them in a large saucepan. Do not completely cover with water. Add the salt and place the cabbage leaf on top of the potatoes. Boil until tender. Drain and remove the cabbage leaf. Place saucepan again over heat, tossing occasionally until the salt forms a crust on the skins.

CHAYOTAS RELLENAS
(Stuffed chayotes in sauce)

You will need:
5 chayotes, 500 grs minced meat, stoned olives, garlic, 1 small glass milk, 1 small piece bread, 2 boiled eggs, black peppercorns, parsley, 1 onion, 3 tomatoes, pimentón, wine, olive oil and salt.

Preparation:

Peel the chayotes and cut them in half, removing the centre. Boil in salted water until tender but not soft and drain.

Prepare the filling as follows: finely chop the parsley, olives and boiled eggs, and crush the garlic. Mix with the minced meat and add the bread, previously soaked in the milk, and 2 or 3 pounded peppercorns. Sauté this mixture in oil in a large pan and fill the chayote halves, reserving a small portion of the filling for the sauce. Place the chayotes, filling up, on kitchen paper, brush with beaten egg and sprinkle with flour.

Fry filled chayotes and skewer each with a cocktail stick to keep the filling in place. Remove from frying-pan and keep warm.

Prepare the sauce as follows: skin and dice the tomatoes, finely chop the onion and pound the garlic.

Place these ingredients in the pan, having removed most of the oil, and cook them together with a teaspoon
of pimentón, a small glass of wine, a cup of water and the unused filling.

Place the chayotes in the sauce and cook for a further four or five minutes.

MORCILLAS
(Black sausage)

You will need:
Pig's blood, 500 grs raisins, 500 grs ground almonds, 500 grs sugar, 250 grs breadcrumbs, aniseed, powdered cinnamon, grated rind of 1 lemon, powdered nutmeg, 2 bunches of parsley, pork fat, skins to fill and some string for tying the sausages.

Preparation:

Put the blood in a "lebrillo" (the large baking bowl mentioned at the beginning of the book), adding the raisins, ground almonds, breadcrumbs, pork fat, sugar, cinnamon, lemon rind, nutmeg, aniseed and finely chopped parsley.

Mix this mass thoroughly. Fill the skins. Tie them well, pierce with a large needle and boil in abundant water.

Drain when cooked and hang to air-dry. These sausages will keep for a long time.

Fry in very hot oil for serving.

ESCACHO
(A potato and gofio mixture)

You will need:
   1 kg potatoes, 1 kg gofio, 250 grs grated dry cheese, green sauce and salt.

Preparation:

   Boil the peeled potatoes in salted water and drain, reserving the water. Mash the potatoes with the green sauce (see page 25). To this liquid mixture add the gofio and grated cheese. Arrange on a serving dish.
   Finely chopped onion can also be added if this dish is to be served immediately.

ESCALDON
(A delicious gofio dish)

You will need:
1/2 kg gofio, 500 grs pork, 1 tomato, 2 potatoes, 1 onion, 3 cloves garlic, thyme, bay leaf, pimentón, oil and salt.

Preparation:

Put the peeled potatoes in a saucepan of water with the chopped pork, the tomato (whole) and the onion (whole), the garlic pounded with a little salt, the thyme, bay leaf, a teaspoon pimentón and half a small glass of oil. Bring to the boil and simmer until the meat is tender and the stock savoury.

Put the gofio in a "lebrillo", add the hot stock and the mashed potatoes and mix well to a stiff consistency. Chop the meat and add to the gofio. Serve with green sauce (see page 25).

This dish can also be prepared with the stock of the "puchero" (see page 11) or any other pottage.

POLINES
(Boiled bananas)

You will need:
Green or slightly ripe bananas, green sauce (see page 25) and salt.

Preparation:

Top and tail the unpeeled bananas. Make a cut lengthwise in the skin. Boil in salted water until tender and drain.

The bananas prepared in this way can be served with green sauce, or sprinkled with sautéd chopped garlic. They can accompany grilled salted fish, with boiled potatoes and a slice of gofio, prepared as follows:

The gofio is mixed to a stiff consistency with water, table salt and olive oil to taste. The mixture is shaped into a ball and cut in slices.

ACEITUNAS CON MOJO
(Olives in garlic dressing)

You will need:

2 kgs olives, 1 head garlic, 1 hot red pepper, pimentón, cumin, parsley, vinegar, olive oil, oregano and thyme.

Preparation:

Wash the olives well and put them in a large screw-top jar. Put the garlic in a mortar with the hot red pepper, the chopped parsley, a little coarse salt, the tip of a teaspoon of cumin and the same amount of pimentón and pound together. Put the contents of the mortar into the jar and add an equal volume each of oil, vinegar and water.

Sprinkle the surface with oregano and thyme and leave to macerate for several days. Shake well before serving.

MOJO COCHINO
(Pork and tripe in dressing)

You will need:
Pig tripe, 500 grs pork, 250 grs bacon, 1 head garlic, 3 onions, 3 tomatoes, cloves, black peppercorns, 1 glass white wine, olive oil, 1/2 hot red pepper, vinegar, pimentón, bay leaf, thyme, oregano, parsley, 150 grs raisins and 150 grs chopped almonds.

Preparation:

Cut the tripe into small portions, fry in oil and place in a saucepan. Repeat this process with the pork and the bacon.

Use this oil to fry also the chopped tomato and onion together with the garlic pounded with the red pepper, 3 black peppercorns and 3 cloves.

To this fried mixture add a teaspoon of pimentón, the glass of white wine, a dash of vinegar and a little water and bring to the boil. Pour over the fried meat, add a little salt, a sprig of thyme, 1 bay leaf, oregano, the raisins and almonds and simmer for a few minutes.

PAPAS CON CARNE
(Potatoes with meat)

You will need:
1 kg pork or veal, 2 kgs potatoes, 2 carrots, 1 onion, 2 tomatoes, 1 head garlic, 1 hot pepper, bay leaf, thyme, pimentón, 1 small glass white wine, oil and salt.

Preparation:

Cut the meat in small pieces, sprinkle lightly with salt and sauté until golden.

Prepare the "fritura" or fried mixture as follows: chop the tomatoes, onion, pepper and garlic and fry together. Add the pimentón, bay leaf, thyme, wine and salt to taste.

Put the meat and the fried mixture into a saucepan with the finely diced carrots and a little water; when half cooked, add the peeled potatoes, cutting large ones in half.

Cook until tender. Add some raisins if desired.

CARNE DE COCHINO EN ADOBO
(Pork in sauce)

You will need:
2 kgs pork, 2 heads garlic, 1 hot red pepper, black peppercorns, pimentón, oil, vinegar, bay leaf, oregano, thyme and salt.

Preparation:

Cut the pork in small pieces.

Prepare the sauce as follows: pound the garlic with the red pepper (previously soaked in hot water), 2 or 3 black peppercorns and salt to taste. Add a teaspoon of pimentón, oregano, bay leaf, thyme, a little oil and a small glass of vinegar.

Mix the meat with the sauce, leave to macerate for at least twelve hours, fry the meat and serve.

CARNE MECHADA
(Stuffed meat)

You will need:

1 2-kg piece beef, 250 grs bacon, 1 onion, 2 heads garlic, parsley, pimentón, oil, 3/4 litre wine, 250 grs ground almonds, cloves, black peppercorns, bay leaf, thyme, salt and a length of string for trussing.

Preparation:

Pound one head of garlic, 2 or 3 peppercorns, cloves, salt, a teaspoon pimentón, several sprigs of parsley and ground almonds together in a mortar.

Tunnel the meat from side to side with a knife or a pair of scissors and thread strips of bacon dipped in the contents of the mortar through these holes.

Truss the roll with string and sauté until golden on all sides.

Put the chopped onion, the other head of garlic (pounded in a mortar), a sprig of thyme, the wine, a little water and salt to taste in a saucepan. Add the meat and cook until tender, turning as often as necessary.

PATA DE COCHINO ASADA
(Roast leg of pork)

You will need:
1 leg of pork, 2 or 3 heads garlic, black peppercorns, juice of 1 lemon, 1 small glass wine, 2 onions, grated nutmeg, pimentón and oregano.

Preparation:

Remove the skin from the leg of pork.

Pound in a mortar the garlic, pimentón, peppercorns, nutmeg, oregano and salt. Add oil, wine and lemon juice.

Macerate the pork overnight with onion rings in the contents of the mortar.

Roast in a hot oven, basting occasionally, until tender.

CONEJO EN SALSA
(Rabbit in sauce)

You will need:
1 rabbit (skinned, cleaned and cut into portions), 2 or 4 dessertspoons red sauce (see page 24), 1 small glass wine, 1 tomato, 1 head garlic, 1 onion, 100 grs almonds, oil, parsley, thyme, oregano and salt.

Preparation:

Sauté the portions of rabbit until golden. Place in a saucepan. Add the red sauce, thyme, oregano and wine.

Add a little of the oil used for frying the rabbit, some water, salt to taste and simmer until the meat is tender and the sauce thickens.

Combine fried diced potatoes before removing from heat.

CONEJO EN SALMOREJO
(Marinated rabbit)

You will need:
1 rabbit (skinned, cleaned and cut into portions), 1 hot red pepper, pimentón, vinegar, oil, cumin, parsley, oregano, thyme and salt.

Preparation:

Leave the rabbit to marinate overnight in a sauce prepared as follows: pound in a mortar the garlic, parsley, oregano, thyme, pimentón and salt to taste, finally adding some oil and vinegar.

Next day fry the rabbit portions, and serve with a cold sauce prepared in the following manner: pound in a mortar the red pepper, 3 cloves garlic, the tip of a teaspoon cumin and salt to taste, finally adding oil and vinegar.

This dish is generally served with "wrinkled potatoes" (see page 32).

CABRITO AL HORNO
(Roast kid)

You will need:
    1 kid (skinned, cleaned and cut into portions), 4 tomatoes, 2 green peppers, 2 heads garlic, 1 leek, parsley, bay leaf, thyme, 2 or 3 black peppercorns, 1/2 glass oil (from previous fry), 2 glasses wine, 1 small glass vinegar and salt.

Preparation:

    Place the portions of kid in an oven dish. Dress with the following mixture: pound together in a mortar the garlic and peppercorns, adding oregano, thyme, bay leaf, and vinegar. (If the meat is marinated in this for twenty-four hours it will be less fatty upon cooking).
    When about to roast, drain off the vinegar, add the salt, peeled and seeded tomatoes, diced green peppers, bay leaf, thyme, chopped parsley and finely chopped leek, some wine and oil, and roast in a moderate oven until tender, basting occasionally.

CABRITO COMPUESTO
(Kid stew)

You will need:
1 kid (skinned, cleaned and cut into portions), 1 glass wine, 1 head garlic, 1/2 small Canarian-style loaf, 100 grs unpeeled almonds, cumin, 7 or 8 black peppercorns, saffron, vinegar and salt.

Preparation:

Marinate the portions of kid with the wine and salt for one hour.

Fry the pieces of meat and put them in a saucepan.

In the same oil fry the garlic, the diced bread and the unpeeled almonds. Pound these fried ingredients in a mortar with a teaspoon of cumin and the peppercorns.

Add to the saucepan together with the oil from the pan, a glass of water, a dash of vinegar and the saffron. Bring to the boil and simmer until the meat is tender.

SANCOCHO
(Salted fish dish)

You will need:
1 1/2 kgs salted fish, 2 kgs potatoes, 1 onion, parsley or fresh coriander and salt.

Preparation:

Shake all excess salt off the fish. Soak for twenty-four hours prior to use, changing the water several times. Drain and cut into portions.

Peel and roughly dice the potatoes and put them in a saucepan of salted water with the fish, some sprigs of parsley or coriander and the whole onion. Bring to the boil and simmer until all the ingredients are tender. Drain and arrange on a serving dish. Serve with red sauce (see page 24) and gofio (see page 30).

COMPUESTO DE LAPAS
(Stuffed limpets)

You will need:
Limpets, breadcrumbs, pimentón, 2 or 3 black peppercorns, parsley, vinegar or lemon juice, oil and salt.

Preparation:

Loosen the limpets from their shells with a knife but do not remove them. Put them, shells down, in a frying-pan and sprinkle with breadcrumbs, finely chopped parsley, 2 or 3 milled peppercorns and a teaspoon of pimentón.

Pour some drops of oil and vinegar or lemon juice over each limpet and salt to taste.

Cook until tender.

CAZUELA
(A fish dish)

You will need:
1 kg fish, 1 kg potatoes, 2 or 3 tomatoes, 1 onion, 1 head garlic, 1 green pepper, oil, fresh coriander or parsley, saffron, mint, pimentón, cumin and salt.

Preparation:

Sauté the chopped onion and tomatoes in oil in a saucepan. Pound the garlic, cumin and salt in a mortar and add to the saucepan with the rounds of green pepper, the chopped coriander or parsley, the saffron, chopped mint, a teaspoon of pimentón and the peeled potatoes cut in two or four according to size.

Add a suitable volume of water, bring to the boil and shortly afterwards add the cleaned and sliced fish. Cook until tender.

Remove the fish and the potatoes from the saucepan and arrange on a serving dish.

The stock can be used for making soup by adding chopped mint and small pieces of toast, or "escaldón" by mixing it, boiling, with gofio (and potatoes, if liked).

Serve the escaldón with green sauce (see page 25).

51

TOLLOS
(A dried fish dish)

You will need:
1 kg dried fish ("tollos"), 1 head garlic, saffron, cumin, oil, vinegar, 1 hot red pepper or chilli, pimentón and salt.

Preparation:

Cut the tollos into small pieces and soak overnight in cold water.

Next day, wash them and put them in a saucepan with water and cook until tender.

Pour off almost all the stock. Add a small glass of oil, another of vinegar, and a pounded mixture of garlic, the tip of a teaspoon of cumin, 1 or 2 threads saffron, a teaspoon pimentón, the chopped chilli or red pepper and salt. Breadcrumbs may be added to the mortar if desired.

Simmer for a few minutes and serve hot.

VIEJAS SANCOCHADAS
(Boiled fish)

You will need:
1 kg fish ("viejas"), 1 onion, 1 tomato, 1 green pepper, 1 lemon, parsley, saffron, oil and salt.

Preparation:

Wash the fish and put into a saucepan of water. Chop the onion, cut the tomato in four and add to the saucepan with 1 or 2 threads of saffron, a sprig of parsley, salt and a little oil.

Bring to the boil and simmer gently until done, taking care not to overcook. Arrange on a serving-dish and garnish with slices of lemon. Serve with "mojo picón" or a vinagrette.

This fine fish is usually accompanied by potatoes, peeled and boiled either with the fish or separately.

COMPUESTO DE SAMA
(Fish in sauce)

You will need:
1 kg fish (in this case "sama"), 2 onions, 2 tomatoes, 1 green pepper, 3 cloves garlic, parsley, cumin, thyme, bay leaf, white wine, oil and salt.

Preparation:

Wash the fish.

Slice the onions, chop the tomatoes and seeded pepper and put into a saucepan with a small glass of wine, the same volume of oil and of water together with a pounded mixture of garlic with salt, parsley and the tip of a teaspoon of toasted cumin.

Arrange the fish in the saucepan, add the bay leaf and a sprig or dash of thyme and cook gently until the fish is done.

PESCADO EN ESCABECHE
(Fish in pickle (hot))

You will need:
1 kg fish, 1/2 small Canarian loaf (hard), 1 head garlic, 1 hot red pepper, 1 teaspoon pimentón, oil, vinegar (or white wine), water, thyme, bay leaf, oregano and salt.

Preparation:

Clean and slice the fish, salt and fry. Arrange fried pieces of fish in a saucepan.

Fry the garlic and croutons in the same oil as the fish. Sprinkle the fried bread with a little vinegar.

Pound the garlic in a mortar with a little salt and a small portion of the hot red pepper, the latter having previously been soaked in hot water. Mix with the fried bread and add to the frying-pan with the oil used for frying the fish, together with the water, pimentón, thyme, bay leaf and oregano. Simmer briefly, pour over the fried fish and boil for a few minutes.

This dish is usually served with "papas arrugadas" (see page 32) or boiled peeled potatoes and is tastier if prepared the day before.

55

PESCADO AL HORNO
(Baked fish)

You will need:
> 1 1/2 kgs fish, 2 onions, 1 green pepper, 1 lemon, wine, oil, salt, parsley, 2 or 3 cloves garlic, thyme, bay leaf and grated nutmeg.

Preparation:

Remove gut and scales from the fish. Leave whole but make some parallel cuts on the sides. Sprinkle with salt.

Cut the pepper and onions in rings and place on a baking tray. Arrange the fish over the rings and garnish with slices of lemon, the chopped or pounded garlic and finely chopped parsley. Pour some oil carefully over the fish and sprinkle with thyme, nutmeg and pieces of bay leaf.

Cook in a hot oven until ready. Serve with boiled potatoes.

PESCADO ENCEBOLLADO
(Fish in onion sauce)

You will need:

2 kgs fish, 3 onions, 1 green pepper, 1 head garlic, 1 dried red pepper (chili), vinegar, oil, salt, thyme, bay leaf, oregano, pimentón, flour, 6 slices dry bread and olives.

Preparation:

Slice, salt and flour the fish.

Fry the chopped garlic and bread slices in olive oil. Boil the dried red pepper, drain and pound in a mortar with the fried garlic and bread.

Fry the fish in the same oil and arrange the pieces in a wide saucepan.

Sauté the chopped onion and green pepper in the same oil. Add the contents of the mortar, a teaspoon of pimentón, a pinch of thyme and of oregano, the bay leaf, a small glass of vinegar and the same volume of water, and simmer on gentle heat for a while.

Add the contents of the frying-pan to the saucepan and cook for a further few minutes.

Arrange on a serving dish and garnish with olives.

FRANGOLLO
(Dessert made with coarse-grained corn flour)

You will need:

500 grs corn flour, 3 litres water, 2 egg yolks, 250 grs sugar, 3 dessertspoons butter, 200 grs raisins, green lemon peel, aniseed, 2 sticks cinnamon and 1 small glass brandy (optional).

Preparation:

Wash the flour carefully in a fine sieve and then place it in a saucepan with the 3 litres of water, the sticks of cinnamon, lemon peel and a dash of aniseed.

Bring slowly to the boil, stirring constantly, until a smooth cream is obtained. Add the raisins, butter, yolks and brandy, beating quickly, and remove from heat.

Pour into a suitable dish and serve (usually cold) with honey or milk.

The flour may be cooked in milk instead of water if preferred.

ARROZ CON LECHE
(Rice pudding)

You will need:

1 cup round-grained rice, 4 cups milk, 4 dessertspoons sugar, green lemon rind, powdered cinnamon and 1 stick cinnamon.

Preparation:

Bring the milk slowly to the boil in a saucepan with the stick of cinnamon and the sugar.

Add the washed rice and the lemon rind and simmer, stirring constantly, until the rice is tender.

Remove the cinnamon sticks and lemon rind, pour into a serving dish and sprinkle with powdered cinnamon.

Noodles can be substituted for the rice in this recipe.

59

CABELLO DE ANGEL
("Angel hair")

You will need:
1 large ripe marrow ("pantana") (with hardened skin), 2 sticks cinnamon and grated lemon rind.

Preparation:

Peel the marrow amd remove the seeds. Cut into large pieces and boil until tender in plenty of water. Drain, chop and wash two or three times, drain well once more and weigh.

Put the marrow into a saucepan with the same weight of sugar, adding the cinnamon sticks, grated lemon rind and two glasses of water (for each kilogram of marrow). Simmer until golden, stirring continuously.

Serve cold.

REBANADAS DE CARNAVAL
(A kind of "French toast")

You will need:
1 or 2 dry Canarian loaves, 1/2 litre milk, 200 grs sugar, 3 eggs, aniseed, grated rind of 1 lemon, oil and powdered cinnamon.

Preparation:

Slice the bread, discarding the ends. Beat the eggs and add the milk, aniseed, lemon rind and cinnamon. Stir well and leave the bread slices to soak briefly. Lift the slices carefully and fry them gently in oil in a frying-pan. Arrange the fried slices on a serving plate and sprinkle with sugar.

An alternative method is to boil the milk with the sugar, a stick of cinnamon and lemon rind. Beat the eggs separately. Dip the slices of bread in the milk and then in the beaten egg and fry.

SOPAS DE MIEL
("Honey soup")

You will need:
2 dry Canarian loaves, 500 grs honey, 250 grs almonds, aniseed, rind of 1 lemon and 1 stick cinnamon.

Preparation:

Toast the almonds and chop them finely. Slice the bread.

Pour the honey into a shallow saucepan with a teaspoon of aniseed and the stick of cinnamon.

Bring this mixture slowly to the boil, add the almonds and the slices of bread. Arrange the soaked slices of bread on a serving dish and pour the honey mixture over them.

Serve cold.

TORTILLAS DE CARNAVAL
("Carnival omelettes" -a kind of pancake)

You will need:

6 eggs, 1/2 litre milk, 250 grs sugar, flour, grated rind of 1 green lemon, aniseed and powdered cinnamon.

Preparation:

Separate the eggs and beat the whites until stiff. Add the sugar gradually, beating constantly.

Add the yolks, milk, grated lemon rind, 1/2 teaspoon of aniseed, the same amount of powdered cinnamon and sufficient flour to achieve a creamy consistency, stirring continually.

Heat a little oil in a frying-pan, spoon in the mixture and fry gently on both sides.

Serve with honey.

TORTAS DE CALABAZA
(Pumpkin patties)

You will need:

250 grs pumpkin, 1 small glass milk, 1 small glass sugar, 2 eggs, grated rind of 1 green lemon, powdered cinnamon and aniseed.

Preparation:

Peel the pumpkin, remove the threads and cut the flesh into largish pieces. Boil in water until tender. Drain and mash with a fork. Add the beaten eggs, milk, sugar, grated lemon rind, cinnamon and aniseed and mix thoroughly.

Heat a little oil together with the rind of 1 orange or lemon in a frying-pan. Fry separate spoonfuls of the mixture on both sides, as minipancakes.

POLVORONES
(A kind of biscuit)

You will need:
500 grs sugar, 500 grs lard, 1 kg flour, powdered cinnamon, grated rind of 1 lemon and powdered aniseed.

Preparation:

Place all the ingredients in a bowl and bind thoroughly with the hands to form a dough.

Take a little of the mixture at a time and flatten to biscuit shape, using both hands.

Place the biscuits on a buttered baking tray and bake until golden.

Another type of biscuit called "mantecado" is prepared by using the same ingredients in identical amounts, but adding 6 beaten eggs and a little salt.

LECHE ASADA
("Roast milk")

You will need:
    1/2 litre milk, 4 eggs, grated rind of 1 green lemon, powdered cinnamon, 3 dessertspoons sugar and a pinch salt.

Preparation:

    Whisk the eggs, add the milk, the lemon rind, a teaspoon of cinnamon, the sugar and a pinch of salt.

    Pour this mixture onto a buttered baking tray and place it, preferably with a water-filled oven tray underneath, in the oven and bake until set.

    This dessert can be further enriched by adding two small tins of condensed milk to the mixture described above.

BUÑUELOS DE QUESO
(Cheese profiteroles)

You will need:
250 grs flour, 100 grs sugar, 250 grs grated dry cheese, 2 eggs and baking powder.

Preparation:

Sieve the flour with the sugar and the baking powder. Add the grated cheese and the beaten eggs and mix to a smooth paste.

Fry spoonfuls of this mixture in abundant hot oil.

Serve with honey or syrup.

67

TORTA DE VILANA
(A spicy loaf)

You will need:

300 grs mashed boiled potatoes, 500 grs sugar, 250 grs flour, 200 grs lard, 1 dessertspoon butter, 2 dessertspoons breadcrumbs, 150 grs ground almonds, 150 grs whole peeled almonds, 8 eggs, 250 grs raisins, powdered cinnamon, grated rind of 1 green lemon, aniseed, 1 sachet baking powder, powdered nutmeg and oil.

Preparation:

Place the eggs, sugar, potatoes and breadcrumbs in a large bowl and knead thoroughly with the hands. Add the ground almonds, the tailed raisins, flour, a little lard, cinnamon, nutmeg, lemon rind, a teaspoon of aniseed, baking powder and butter and knead the mixture further. The dough should be of intermediate consistency.

Line a high cake tin with brown or greaseproof paper and then grease the paper well with lard and a little oil, spinkling finally with flour. Extend the dough, keeping the surface level as low as possible to avoid spilling over in the oven. Decorate with the halved or whole peeled almonds.

68

Put the tray into the centre of the oven. The initial temperature should be suitably high, but once the dough has risen the temperature of the oven can be lowered. Bake for approximately one hour. Check that the loaf is ready by piercing the centre with a skewer, which should come out dry.

MARQUESOTES
(Pieces of cake, soaked in syrup)

You will need:
5 eggs, 300 grs sugar, 300 grs flour, baking powder, grated rind of 1 green lemon and powdered cinnamon.
Syrup: 200 grs sugar and 1/2 glass water.

Preparation:

Separate the eggs and whisk the whites until stiff. Add the sugar and then the yolks, beating constantly.

Mix in the sieved flour, baking powder and cinnamon and work to a smooth creamy consistency.

Grease a cake tin with butter and pour in the dough. Place in the centre of a hot oven. Check that the cake is ready by piercing with a skewer, which should come out dry. Turn out onto a wire rack.

Meanwhile, to prepare the syrup, boil 1/2 cup of water with 200 grs sugar and the lemon rind, stirring continually until slightly golden and all the sugar has dissolved.

Cut the cake into diamond-shaped pieces and pour the syrup over them.

The pieces of cake can alternatively be decorated with meringue: beat egg whites until stiff, adding a dessertspoon of sugar for each one, spread over the pieces of cake and put back into the (low) oven until the meringue has dried.

BIZCOCHÓN
(Plain cake)

You will need:

6 eggs, 2 cups sugar, slightly less than 2 cups flour, 1/2 cup oil, 1/2 cup milk, 1 sachet baking powder, grated rind of 1 green lemon and powdered cinnamon.

Preparation:

Separate the eggs and whip the whites until stiff. Add the yolks and then the sugar, beating continually. Fold in the sieved flour and add the oil and milk.

Mix in the lemon rind, baking powder and cinnamon.

Butter a cake tin, spoon in the mixture and place in the oven. Check after about 40 minutes that the cake is ready by piercing with a skewer, which should come out dry.

Turn out on a wire rack and leave to cool.

PAN DE ALMENDRAS
(Almond bread)

You will need:

500 grs ground almonds, 750 grs sugar, 250 grs flour, 6 eggs, 1 litre milk, 1 teaspoon baking powder, powdered aniseed, powdered cinnamon and the grated rind of 1 green lemon.

Preparation:

Put the ground almonds, sugar, beaten eggs and milk in a baking bowl and beat thoroughly. Fold in the sieved flour and continue to beat, finally adding the aniseed, cinnamon, baking powder and lemon rind.

Butter a cake tin, spoon in the mixture and bake in a hot oven until golden.

QUESADILLAS
(Cheesecake)

You will need:
   1 kg unsalted soft cheese, 250 grs flour, 500 grs sugar, 3 eggs, powdered cinnamon, grated rind of 1 green lemon and aniseed.

Preparation:

   Grate the cheese and mix with the sugar, flour and beaten eggs. Add the cinnamon, lemon rind and a teaspoon of aniseed and beat well.

   Mix the flour and a little water to make a light dough. Turn out onto a floured board and roll to pie-lining thickness. Grease a pastry tin and line with the pastry, fill with the cheese mixture and bake until golden in a hot oven.

TRUCHAS
(Sweet potato pasties)

You will need:
Filling: 500 grs sweet potatoes, 250 grs ground almonds, 1 small glass fine or castor sugar, 3 egg yolks, grated rind of 1 green lemon, anisette (liqueur), rum, powdered aniseed and powdered cinnamon.
Pastry: 3 dessertspoons lard, 1 small glass olive oil and 500 grs flour.

Preparation:

Filling: Boil, peel and mash the sweet potatoes and mix with the ground almonds, lemon rind, sugar, yolks, a dash each of anisette and rum, and a teaspoon each of powdered aniseed and cinnamon.

Pastry: Mix the lard, oil and flour to a consistency suitable for pastry. Leave for half an hour, then roll out thinly on a floured board. Cut out saucer-sized circles, place some filling on one side, flip over the other side to cover, press the edges together and flute with a fork to decorate. Pierce one side of each trucha lightly with a fork.

Finally, fry pasties in abundant hot oil, drain on kitchen paper, sprinkle with sugar and arrange on serving dish.

These pasties will keep well in an airtight tin.

QUESO DE ALMENDRAS
(Almond cheese)

You will need:

500 grs ground almonds, 500 grs sugar, 8 yolks, 3 egg whites, grated rind of 1 green lemon, powdered cinnamon and 1/4 litre water.

Preparation:

Warm the water in a saucepan, add the sugar and stir until a golden syrup is formed. Remove from the heat.

Beat the egg whites, fold in the yolks and mix well. Add this to the saucepan and bring to the boil. Lower the heat and mix in the ground almonds, lemon rind and a quarter of a teaspoon of powdered cinnamon.

Stir over gentle heat to avoid sticking. The mixture is ready when it comes away from the sides of the saucepan. Remove from heat and turn into a buttered mould. Leave to cool.

ALMENDRADOS
(Almond biscuits)

You will need:
1 kg ground almonds, 1 kg sugar, 5 eggs, grated rind and juice of 1 green lemon, powdered cinnamon and lard.

Preparation:

Put the ingredients into a baking bowl in the following order: almonds, sugar, beaten eggs, lemon rind, lemon juice and a teaspoon of powdered cinnamon.

Mix thoroughly to a firm paste, shape into round, flat biscuits and place on a greased baking tray. Bake in a hot oven until crisp and golden.

BIENMESABE
(Almond dessert)

You will need:

500 grs ground almonds, 750 grs sugar, 1/2 litre water, 8 yolks, powdered cinnamon and the grated rind of 1 green lemon.

Preparation:

Prepare a syrup as follows: warm the water in a saucepan, add the sugar and bring to the boil. Simmer until golden, stirring constantly. Add the almonds, lemon rind and cinnamon. Continue stirring over gentle heat until the mixture thickens.

Leave to cool, add 8 beaten yolks, mix thoroughly and bring to the boil again.

Spoon into individual dishes and serve cold.

Note: The almonds may be peeled and toasted rather than ground.

RAPADURAS
(Almond and honey sweetmeats)

You will need:
1 litre sugarcane syrup, 500 grs sugar, 250 grs ground almonds (which may be toasted before grinding), grated rind of 1 green lemon, aniseed, powdered cinnamon and gofio (a locally made corn or wheat flour, toasted).

Preparation:

Put the following ingredients in a saucepan over gentle heat: syrup, sugar, cinnamon, lemon rind and aniseed.

Bring to the boil, stirring continually. Remove from heat and continue stirring. When the mixture has set, add the almonds and the gofio and blend thoroughly to form a stiff paste.

Butter conical aluminium moulds and fill with the mixture.

Leave to cool and remove gently from the moulds.

GOFIO DE ALMENDRAS
(Gofio with almonds)

You will need:
2 kgs gofio (1 kg each of corn and wheat), 500 grs honey, 250 grs lard, grated rind of 5 lemons, 500 grs ground almonds and 1/4 litre wine.

Preparation:

Toast the almonds in a frying-pan together with the lemon rind, but do not overcook to avoid the lemon flavour becoming bitter.

Add the wine and an equal volume of water to this paste. Place over gentle heat and stir with a wooden spoon. Finally, add the honey, lard and gofio, stirring continually.

Remove from heat and leave to cool. Shape into little balls (golf ball size), which will keep well in an airtight tin.

GALLETAS DE NATA
(Cream biscuits)

You will need:

1 cup cream from either cows- or goatsmilk (or tinned cream), 2 kgs flour, 500 grs sugar, 1 cup lard, 1/2 cup oil, 1 packet butter, 6 yolks, 3 egg whites, powdered cinnamon, 1 dessertspoon aniseed, grated rind of 1 green lemon and 1 dessertspoon baking-soda.

Preparation:

Mix all the ingredients thoroughly in a large baking bowl.

Roll out the dough thus obtained on a floured board to a thickness of 1/4 inch. Cut into rounds or squares, as desired.

Line a baking tray with greased paper and bake in a moderate oven until golden.

ARROPE
(Grape liqueur)

You will need:
Crude liquid from pressed grapes (known locally as "mosto").

Preparation:

This tasty liqueur is prepared by simmering the mosto until concentrated, which may take quite some time. Stir occasionally to avoid sticking to the saucepan.

Remove from heat and leave to cool.

This liqueur can be mixed with gofio and shaped into little balls.

MEJUNJE
(Rum and mint liqueur)

You will need:
1 litre rum, 250 grs brown sugar, 5 dessertspoons honey, 2 slices of green lemon, powdered cinnamon and a sprig of mint.

Preparation:

Mix the rum with the sugar until the latter is dissolved. Add the mint leaves, honey, lemon slices and a teaspoon of cinnamon. Pour into a large jar and close tightly.

Leave for one week and then filter. Bottle the liqueur with a few mint leaves.

HUEVOS ESPIRITUALES
(Literally, "spiritual eggs")

You will need:
2 yolks, 1/2 litre old wine or schnapps ("aguardiente"), 100 grs sugar, grated rind of half a lemon and powdered cinnamon.

Preparation:

Whisk the eggs, gradually adding the wine, sugar, cinnamon and lemon rind.

When the sugar has been dissolved, heat gently. Stir constantly and remove just before boiling.

Serve cold.

LICOR DE RUDA
(Aromatic plant liqueur)

You will need:

1 kg sugar, 1 litre aguardiente, 1/2 litre water, 2 or 3 sprigs of the plant "ruda", rind of 1 lemon and powdered cinnamon.

Preparation:

Mix the ruda, aguardiente, lemon rind and cinnamon in a large glass container and stopper tightly. Leave for ten days.

Then prepare a thick syrup as follows: boil 1 kg of sugar in 1/2 litre of water until thick and golden, leave to cool, pour into the liquid in the jar, mix well, filter and bottle.

LICOR DE CAFE
(Coffee liqueur)

You will need:
500 grs ground coffee, 1 litre aguardiente, 3/4 litre water, 750 grs sugar and a sprig of "reina luisa".

Preparation:

Mix the coffee with the aguardiente and reina luisa in a large glass container. Stopper and leave for two weeks.

Then prepare a syrup as follows: boil the sugar and water until thick and golden, leave to cool, pour into the liquid in the glass container and leave for a further two weeks.

Filter and bottle.

LICOR DE LECHE
(Milk liqueur)

You will need:
1 litre pure alcohol, 1 kg sugar, 1 litre milk, 1 glass water, 3 slices lemon and 1 stick cinnamon.

Preparation:

Prepare a thick syrup with the water and sugar as described earlier. Leave to cool. Then add the milk, alcohol, lemon slices and cinnamon.

Pour into a large glass container and stopper and leave for two weeks. Filter and bottle.

MISTELA
(Orange liqueur)

You will need:
1 litre aguardiente or caña (spirit from sugar cane), finely peeled rind of 4 locally grown oranges, 1 or 2 sachets aniseed, 2 sticks cinnamon, 1 litre water and 1 kg sugar.

Preparation:

Mix the aguardiente, orange rind, cinnamon and aniseed and pour into a large glass container. Stopper and leave for approximately 15 days.

Prepare the syrup with the litre of water and the sugar, as described earlier. Leave to cool and pour into the liquid in the glass container. Filter and bottle.

LICOR DE BERROS
(Watercress liqueur)

You will need:
    1 litre aguardiente or pure alcohol, 250 grs watercress, 1 kg sugar and 1/2 water.

Preparation:

    Wash the watercress thoroughly.

    Put the watercress and aguardiente into a large glass container and close tightly. Leave for one week.

    Prepare a syrup with the water and sugar as described earlier. Leave to cool and then add to the filtered contents of the container.

    Bottle and leave for several days before serving.

INDEX

CENTRE OF CANARIAN POPULAR CULTURE

The Centre of Canarian Popular Culture (CCPC) is an Autonomus Cultural Movement, the objectives of which ar e to promote and develop all aspects of Canarian culture throughout the entire archipelago.

The current basic task of the CCPC is to collaborate with civic associations as well as public and private Institutions in organising cultural activities, editing books, records and tapes and generally promoting any groups or individual persons who endeavour to disseminate the culture of the Canary Islands.

In order to better achieve its objectives, the CCPC will represent its members in all matters concerning cultural organisations and initiatives in programming activities of an exclusively cultural nature.

Members of the CCPC include representatives of the areas of folklore, theatre, music, cinema, photography, poetry, comedy, art exhibitions and lectures.

Our doors are open to all who wish to cooperate in achieving the ends described above and our addresses are as follows:

TENERIFE: C/Molinos de Agua, 47 bajo (Barrio Nuevo), La Laguna. Telephone: 258408.

GRAN CANARIA: C/Pedro de Vera, 7 bajo, Las Palmas. Telephone: 372730